D0921995

Lemon

or

Lemonade

by Laurie Lynn Davis

Listen and sing along with Sally Mae by scanning this QR code or by going to www.sallymaebooks.org.

Illustrated by
Trevor Shackleton and Monika Clifton

U.S. Copyright: TXus2-138-396

ISBN: 978-1-7338777-0-1

Dedication:

This book is dedicated to my sister-in-law Chree.

As she faced cancer and treatments

with all the horrible side effects,

she chose joy over sorrow,

making lemonade from lemons.

Thank you for your inspiration!

"Ms. Robin! Ms. Robin!

Look at the little pumpkins!"

"Yes, Sally Mae,
they are starting to grow
and we all appreciate
your diligence of keeping
our pumpkin seeds
watered this summer.

Your Grandpa Greg was very kind to donate the **seeds** and his time to make our class garden beautiful this fall.'

"Girls, don't forget
to **take a picture**
of the little pumpkins
for your book."

"OK, Ms. Robin,"
Ann and I echoed together.
We were the garden helpers
and allowed to work
in the class garden
during recess time.

For the next few weeks we saw the pumpkins grow
from little green pumpkins
to larger green colored pumpkins.
We kept taking pictures
and were excited to share
our pumpkin book
with the class.

We had listed all the stages of the
pumpkins' life cycle.
We had taken pictures from the beginning
when Grandpa Greg, Ann and I
had planted the seeds.
We had pictures and information
on the seed, seedling, vine,
yellow flower,
small green pumpkins,
and larger green pumpkins.

We just needed **one** more picture
to finish our book.

Pumpkin Life Cycle

seed

sprout

vine

flower

green pumpkin

orange pumpkin

Ms. Robin came over to us
during the writing station time
to see how we were doing on our book.

"We are almost done Ms. Robin. We just need
our pumpkins to turn orange!"

"Girls, you are doing a **great job**.
I heard this weekend
we should have some nice weather.
Let's see what they look like on Monday."

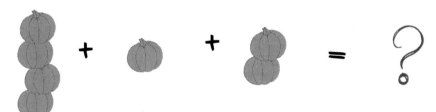

Over the weekend,
Ann and I talked about our book
and how we would share the pumpkins
with the class
for a fun **pumpkin math** project.
Plus, we would get to roast
the pumpkin seeds. YUM!

Instead of seeing
our beautiful orange pumpkins
we saw smashed pumpkins all over.
Someone had **ripped off**
the rest of the pumpkins from the vine.
They were all **gone.**
The pumpkins were **smashed.**

Tears came to our eyes
as we went to get Ms. Robin
before school started
to show her what had happened.

"Ms. Robin! Ms. Robin!
Did you see the garden?"

"Oh girls, I saw the garden this morning
and was SO **disappointed**
that someone would steal the pumpkins
and vandalize the class garden."

While we were talking to Ms. Robin,
the rest of the class started to arrive at school
and noticed the garden.
Everyone was **sad**
because they were looking forward
to seeing the orange pumpkins.

Ms. Robin called
our custodian, Ms. Janet
to **clean up** the mess
and said
we could help her throw away
the smashed pumpkins.
Sadly, we cleaned up
the mess of the garden together.

Ms. Janet came over to us and said
*"I'm so **sorry** girls.*
*I have seen **all** the work*
that you have done with the pumpkins.
I don't understand
why people vandalize.
*However, I want to **share** a song with*
you that my Mom taught me
when I was young.
Would you like to hear it?"

"*OK*," Ann and I said together.
Ms. Janet started to sing:

Lemon or Lemonade?

What will you choose?

BITTER or BETTTER?

What will you do?

Will you choose lemon and be sour too?
Or add some sugar and make it sweet?

Lemon or lemonade?

BITTER or BETTER?
SOUR or SWEET?

What will you choose?

What will you do?

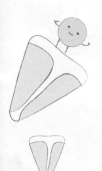

We both looked at her with sad **puzzled** looks on our faces.

What do lemons have to do with our pumpkins?

She smiled and said,
"What does a lemon taste like?"
"Oh, it's sour!
I tried one and didn't like it" said Ann.

"Well girls, have you had lemonade?"

"Oh ya! We love lemonade."

"Ann, remember when we set up a lemonade stand outside in the summer?
My mom showed us how to make FRESH lemonade!"

"So girls, do you remember how you made it?"

"YES!

First, we **squeezed** the lemons and got the juice.

Next, we **added** sugar and water and stirred it all up.

Last, we added some *ice* cubes to keep it nice and cold."

"That's right girls.
Now, look at the smashed pumpkins
and missing pumpkins.
How are you feeling?"

We both said, *"Sad"* together.
Ann added and, *"I'm mad too!"*

"Girls, you have to make a choice.
Do you want to stay sad and mad
or do you want to remember
all the FUN TIMES you had with this garden?
Do you want to be bitter about this situation?
That means staying upset
and remaining angry
or do you want to **remember** the better
times you had in the garden?"

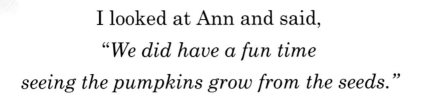

I looked at Ann and said,
*"We did have a fun time
seeing the pumpkins grow from the seeds."*

Ann nodded her head in agreement.
We looked back at Ms. Janet
and said together,
*"We choose to remember
the **better** times."*

"Great CHOICE girls.
Thanks for helping me
clean up the mess.
Have a great day."

The next morning at school,
Ms. Robin told us that Ms. Janet
wanted to talk to our class.
She smiled
as she went to the front of the class.

"Yesterday,
I helped Sally Mae and Ann
clean up the pumpkin mess
and we talked about how they were feeling.
They both were feeling sad and mad.
But, they made a **decision**
to remember the **good times**
they had in the garden and to NOT stay angry."

"I was **so touched**
when I heard the girl's decision
that I called my parents
who own a PUMPKIN PATCH
and told them about the situation at school."
"Guess what they said to me?"

"They **invited** your entire class
to come to their pumpkin patch
and pick out your own pumpkins.
Plus, they want you to go on a HAYRIDE
and enjoy some fresh APPLE CIDER
How does that sound?"

"Yay!" "Cool!" "Awesome!"

The entire class started to clap and cheer.

Ms Robin said, *"Let's all say THANK YOU to Ms. Janet for this wonderful news."*

"Thank you Ms. Janet" echoed the entire class.

I looked at Ann
who was grinning from ear to ear.
We would be able
to get a picture of a large
orange pumpkin after all.
It didn't turn out
how I thought it would,
but it turned out to be better
for the entire class.

Hmmm...I thought to myself
I'm glad Ann and I
chose to remember
the better things about the garden

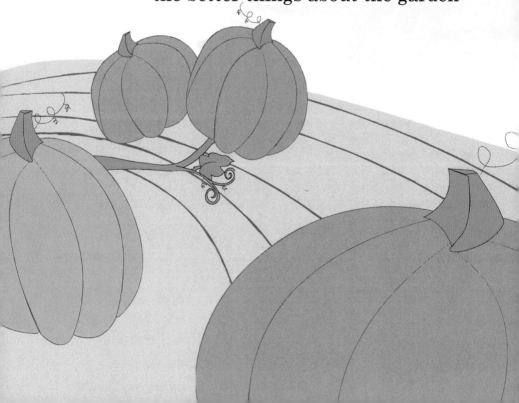

I **smiled** to myself and pictured each of us holding a large orange pumpkin.

Bitter or better?

I'm glad we chose BETTER!

The End

THANKS

for reading and singing along with Sally Mae
and her friends.

Now, please talk with a partner and share
about a time when you had to make a decision
about choosing to be bitter or better about a situation
Did you choose lemons or lemonade?

Made in the USA
Middletown, DE
26 August 2022

72244144R00020